SPRINGS

ANGELA ROYSTON

www.heinemann.co.uk.
Visit our website to find out more information about Heinemann Library books

To order:
☎ Phone ++44 (0)1865 888066
🖷 Send a fax to ++44 (0)1865 314091
💻 Visit the Heinemann Bookshop at www.heinemann.co.uk to browse our catalogue and order online.

First published in Great Britain by Heinemann Library,
Halley Court, Jordan Hill, Oxford OX2 8EJ,
a division of Reed Educational and Professional Publishing Ltd.
Heinemann is a registered trademark of Reed Educational & Professional Publishing Limited.

OXFORD MELBOURNE AUCKLAND
JOHANNESBURG BLANTYRE GABORONE
IBADAN PORTSMOUTH NH (USA) CHICAGO

© Reed Educational and Professional Publishing Ltd 2000

The moral right of the proprietor has been asserted.

Designed by Visual Image
Illustrations by Barry Atkinson
Originated by Dot Gradations
Printed in Hong Kong/China

04 03 02 01 00
10 9 8 7 6 5 4 3 2 1

ISBN 0431 01745 X

British Library Cataloguing in Publication Data

Royston, Angela
  Springs. - (How it works)
  1.Springs (Mechanism) - Juvenile literature
  I.Title
  621.8'24

Acknowledgements

The Publishers would like to thank the following for permission to reproduce photographs: Cumulus: Trevor
Clifford pp4, 12, 14, 15, 21; Greg Evans International Photo Library: Greg Balfour Evans p8; Heinemann:
Trevor Clifford pp5, 7, 11, 16, 18, 20, 24, 28, 29; Reylon: p10; Sporting Pictures (UK) Ltd: p9, p23; Tony Stone
Images: Bob Torrez p22, p26; TRHMcDonnell Douglas Corp: p19

Cover photograph reproduced with permission of Science Photo Library.

The Publishers would like to thank Anthony Mirams for his help and advice with the text and Jo Brooker for
making the models on p28-9.

Every effort has been made to contact copyright holders of any material reproduced in this book. Any
omissions will be rectified in subsequent printings if notice is given to the Publisher.

Any words appearing in the text in bold, **like this**, are explained in the Glossary.

CONTENTS

What are springs?

A spring can be long and tight, wide and loose or even flat. Can you tell which of these springs have been made to be stretched rather than squashed?

Most springs are made from **coiled** pieces of metal. They are used in toys, in furniture, in cameras, video players and many other **machines**. Springs are useful because, when they are stretched or squashed, they try to bounce back into shape.

A spring is a simple machine. It is so simple that you probably do not think of it as a machine at all. **Levers**, wheels, springs, ramps and pulleys are also simple machines. This book shows how springs work and how they are used.

Make it work!

Experiment with a Slinky. What happens when the steps are very deep? What happens when the step is very wide? Why does the Slinky sometimes not go all the way down the stairs?
Why won't the Slinky go upstairs?

When one end of the Slinky is pulled down to the step below, the rest of the Slinky follows. Why does the end jump over the spring onto the next step below?

Slinky

A Slinky is a spring that goes downstairs on its own. When the top is stretched from one step to the step below, the coils try to return to their correct shape. This stretches the next few coils, and so on, to the end of the spring. As the last coil moves forwards and down, it carries on moving and drops onto the next step below. The whole cycle is then repeated.

Jack-in-a-box

squashed spring

To shut the box of a jack-in-a-box you have to push the clown inside and shut the catch. Inside the clown is a large spring.

A jack-in-a-box can make you jump if you are not expecting it to bounce out. When the lid of the box is shut, the spring inside the clown is **compressed**. This means that the **coils** of the spring are pushed together and the spring takes up less room.

The spring tries to return to its usual shape and pushes up against the lid. The lid has to have a strong catch to keep it shut. When the lid is opened, the spring bounces out of the box.

Make it work!

Wind a piece of thin wire around a pencil so that it looks like a coiled spring. Remove the pencil. Now you have a spring. Squash it and then let go. What happens? Stretch it a little and then let go. What happens? How far can you stretch it before it begins to lose its shape?

When this lid is opened, the spring bounces back and the snake jumps up.

How a spring works

You have to use **energy** to force something to change shape. The important thing about a spring is that when it is compressed or stretched, it stores that energy. Then, when the force is no longer acting on it, it uses the energy it has stored to bounce back into shape. If something is attached to the spring, then the stored energy will move it too.

Soft landing

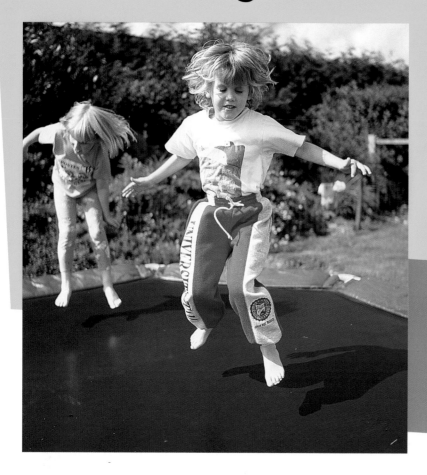

A trampoline gives people an extra upwards push with each bounce.

When you jump on a trampoline, the canvas gives way and helps you to bounce up again. It is not the canvas that is stretching, but the springs that hold it to the frame. Watch the springs as someone else jumps up and down. Can you see them stretching and **relaxing**? As the stretched springs relax, their **energy** gives the trampoliner an extra boost.

Springs are not the only things that bounce back into shape. Foam mattresses are used in the gym and in athletics to give a soft landing. The foam squashes under your weight, like a spring. It gives back some energy, but not as much energy as a trampoline does.

Why does a ball bounce?

When a rubber ball hits the ground, it is squashed out of shape. The rubber stores the energy. As the ball returns to its round shape, the energy is released and pushes the ball up into the air.

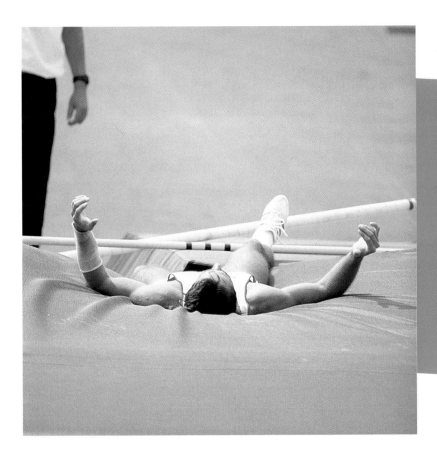

A pole vaulter skims over the bar and lands on the foam mattress. The foam squashes under his weight to give him a safe, soft landing.

Make it work!

Test different balls to see how bouncy they are. Drop them onto the ground and then measure the height they bounce back up to. You may need a partner to help you. Why do some balls bounce higher than others?

Sitting comfortably

The springs inside a mattress compress to support your weight.

The mattress on your bed probably has springs inside it. They **compress** and **relax** under your weight to help you sleep more comfortably. A mattress on the floor is fun to jump on. Why do you think the springs of a trampoline give you back more **energy** than the springs of the mattress?

Settees and easy chairs often have springs inside them too. They are usually bigger than bed springs and there are not so many of them. This is because all your weight is concentrated in one area when you sit down.

Make it work!

Draw a design for a chair which uses springs to let the back tilt back. Your drawing should show how springs let the back move backwards and then upright. Use springs to make the chair comfortable too.

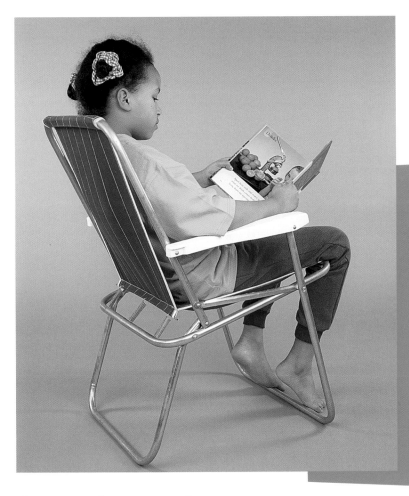

The springs in this chair join the soft material that you sit on to the hard metal frame. When you sit down, the springs stretch and the material gives under your weight.

Stretchy springs

Some chairs have springs that stretch when you sit on them. When a spring is stretched, it is said to be in **tension**. The energy in a **tense** spring pushes back against your weight so that you sit more comfortably.

Shut the door!

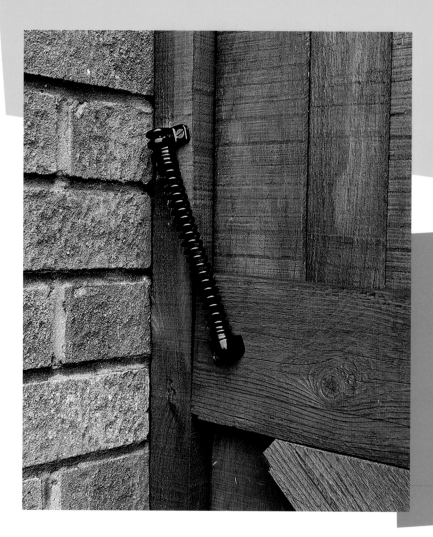

This spring closes the door when it has been opened. Where would you fix the spring if you wanted it to keep the door open?

Some doors and gates have a spring to make sure they cannot be left open. The spring stretches when you open the door. As soon as you let go of the door, the spring tightens again, pulling the door closed.

Some doors have a doorstop on the wall behind to stop them hitting the wall. When you push the door wide open, the spring stops it hitting the wall. The spring absorbs some of the shock of the door banging against it.

Door catch

A door handle uses two springs to open and close the catch. The handle is attached to the top spring. As the handle turns, it pushes a plate which pulls back a bolt. As the bolt moves back, it tightens the lower spring and pulls back the catch. When you let the door handle go, the springs **relax** and release the catch.

plate

bolt

springs

catch open

catch closed

The spring on the handle and the spring on the catch work together to open and shut the catch. The catch fits into a slot on the door frame.

Umbrella and pen

This small umbrella opens quickly and easily. When you press the catch on the handle, it shoots open.

Most umbrellas use a spring of some kind, but the springiest umbrellas are the small pocket kind that spring open when you press the button to release the catch. A spring in the handle pushes the **mechanism** up the stem. The mechanism opens up the **spokes** to spread the umbrella out. When the rain stops, you slide the mechanism back down the stem. The umbrella collapses and folds and the stem folds like a **telescope** into the handle. The spring inside is squashed and held in place by the catch.

Spring-loaded pen

Pens with a button at the end, have a spring inside. When you press the button down, it pushes out the tip and stretches the spring. The spring tries to pull the tip inside again, but it cannot because it is held by a catch. Pushing the button releases the catch and the tip springs back.

Weighing machines

When you put the fruit on the scales, the spring inside stretches and the needle shows how heavy the fruit is.

A spring balance is a weighing machine which has a spring inside. The heavier the weight, the more the spring stretches.
Apples that weigh 4 kilograms, for example, stretch the spring twice as far as 2 kilograms of apples, and four times as far as 1 kilogram.

The spring inside a weighing machine is so strong it only moves a little when you weigh something. But it is attached to a needle that moves around a dial. The needle moves further than the spring to show how much the object weighs.

16

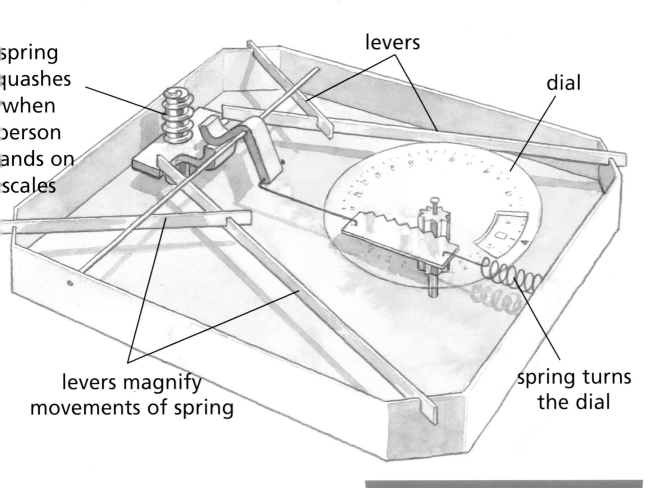

spring squashes when person stands on scales

levers

dial

levers magnify movements of spring

spring turns the dial

Bathroom scales

The spring inside bathroom scales is even smaller and stronger than that in a spring balance. **Levers** inside the bathroom scales change the small movement of the spring into a much larger movement of the needle on the dial.

The springs inside weighing machines are so stiff they only move a small distance even for a heavy weight.

Make it work!

Use a spring balance to measure the weight of different things. Make a chart to show how heavy each thing is.

Elastic bands

Can you spot how many ways this girl is taking advantage of the stretchiness of elastic and rubber bands?

Elastic bands are made of rubber. Elastic stretches and returns to shape just like a spring. It is used in some clothes to make them easy to get on and off. The top of the trousers stretch to let you pull them up and then **relaxes** to fit around your waist.

Rubber bands are used to hold things together, such as cards or envelopes. The more you stretch the band the tighter it pulls. But, if you stretch it too much, it will snap.

An aircraft needs to be going very fast to take off into the air. The deck is not long enough for the plane to reach the speed it needs, so it is given an extra push by a huge catapult.

Catapults

A catapult uses a rubber band to propel a small wad of paper forward. As the band is pulled back, it stores **energy**, like a spring. When it is released, the energy pushes the paper forward. A huge catapult is used on the deck of an aircraft carrier. When a plane takes off, it is given extra speed by the catapult.

Make it work!

Make a board like this one. Use it to catapult a model car forward. Measure how far back you pull the rubber band.
Does the distance you stretch the rubber band affect how far the car goes?

Clockwork

Some toys use a **clockwork mechanism** to make them move in different ways. When the clockwork frog is wound up and released, it jumps across the floor. Inside the frog is a spring. With most clockwork cars you have to pull them backwards across the floor to wind up the spring. When you let it go, the spring unwinds and turns **cog wheels** inside the car. The cog wheels turn the wheels.

This boy is using a key to wind up a clockwork train. Can you guess how each of these clockwork toys will move when they are wound up?

20

When you turn
the key on a
wind-up clock, it
tightens the large
spiral spring. As
it unwinds it
releases energy
to make the
clock work.

Wind-up clock

The same kind of spring is used inside old-fashioned clocks and watches. When the large clockwork spring is wound up, it becomes a store of **energy**. As it slowly unwinds it moves a series of cog wheels. One of the cog wheels is attached to the hour hand and another to the minute hand.

Make it work!

Make a spiral spring. Take a long, thin strip of paper and wrap it around a pencil as shown here. Remove the pencil. What happens to the paper?

Springboards

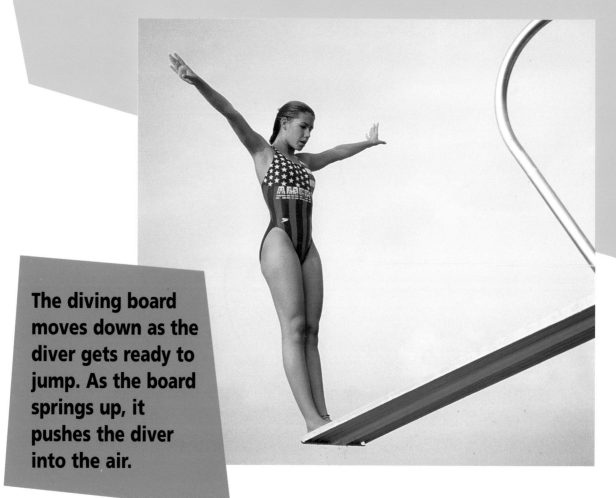

The diving board moves down as the diver gets ready to jump. As the board springs up, it pushes the diver into the air.

When a long, thin piece of wood bends, it acts as a spring. Divers use this fact when they jump off a diving board. When the diver bounces on the end of the board, the board bends down. As the diver begins to jump, the board returns to its original shape, like a spring.

A heavy person bends the springboard more than a light person. But it takes a bigger push to lift a heavy person and so the board lifts all divers by the same amount.

Make it work!

Use a wooden or plastic ruler as a catapult. Draw a target on a large piece of cardboard. Screw up some small pieces of paper. Wet the pieces of paper and then flick them with the ruler towards the target. You can see where the paper hits the target by the wet patch it leaves. Can you hit the centre of the target?

The springiness of the bow powers the arrow through the air towards the target.

Bow and arrow

An archer with a bow can shoot an arrow through the air further and faster than he could throw it. As the arrow is pulled back, the bow bends and stores the **energy** of the pull, like a spring. When the bow is released, the energy passes to the arrow. The arrow flies through the air. The bow moves a small way to push the arrow a long way.

23

Flat springs

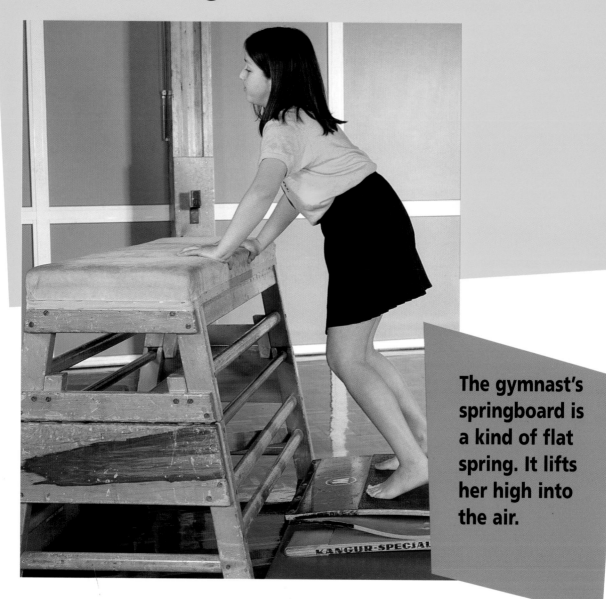

The gymnast's springboard is a kind of flat spring. It lifts her high into the air.

Gymnasts use a springier board than a diver. The board is made springier because it uses three pieces of wood joined one on top of the other. The gymnast jumps on to the board heavily. All three parts of the board bend, increasing the amount of **energy** stored. As the board unbends, she is given a large extra push.

spring

This old carriage has flat springs laid one on top of the other to give the driver and passengers a more comfortable ride over the bumps in the road.

Leaf springs

A **leaf spring** is several flat metal springs laid one on top of the other and held together with bands. These springs are used in cars and are very strong. They are slightly curved so that they become straight when the car is carrying a heavy load. As the wheels bump over the road, the springs bend to absorb the sudden jolts of energy and then **relax** to release it more smoothly.

Make it work!

Draw a design for a springboard that would help you jump really high. Use whatever kind of springs you like. Can you think of anything that your spring board could be useful for, such as picking apples from the top of the tree?

A comfortable ride

Motor-cross riders race their bikes over muddy, bumpy ground. The fastest one around the course is the winner. As the bike goes over a large bump, it takes off and lands with a jolt. The bike has long springs between the handlebars and the front wheel. They **compress** when the bike hits the ground to give a softer landing for the rider.

The motor-cross bike flies through the air. What do you think the springs are for?

The coiled spring and shock absorber protect the people in the car from the jolts and bumps on the road.

Shock absorbers

shock absorber

piston

If you have ever driven a go-kart you will know that you feel every bump it goes over. When cars and other vehicles drive along the road, their wheels vibrate too. But the force of the jolts is absorbed by springs and **shock absorbers**.

The spring compresses and **relaxes** to even out the jolts and make the drive more comfortable. The piston of the shock absorber moves in and out to take some of the **energy** from the spring.

Make a jack-in-a-box

You can make your own spring to put in this jack-in-the-box.

You will need:

- a gift box or large clean yoghurt carton
- a piece of strong, bendy garden wire six times as long as the depth of the box or carton
- masking tape
- clean, old socks
- glue and scraps of material
- 2 thick rubber bands
- a broom handle

1 Wind the wire around the broom handle to make a spring which is a bit longer than the depth of your box or carton.

2 Stuff the toe of one of the socks with the other socks to make the head of the snake. Twist a rubber band around the sock just below the head.

3 Cut out pieces of material to make eyes and the tongue of the snake. Stick them onto the head.

4 Bend one end of the spring upright and push it inside the head. Pull the sock down over the spring.

5 Bend the other end of the spring into the centre and stick it to the bottom of the box or carton using masking tape.

6 Push the snake down into the box and close the lid. Hold it in place with the second rubber band.

7 When you open the lid, the snake will spring out!

Glossary

bolt a metal rod which fits into a hole or a nut

clockwork machinery that makes something move by winding up a spring

cog wheel a wheel with teeth cut around the edge

coiled wound round and round in a circle

compressed squashed

cycle something that repeats itself

energy the ability to make something move

force a push, pull or twist that makes something move

leaf spring flat spring used in cars and carriages

lever a simple machine that is used to lift or balance something

machine a device that allows you to do something more easily or that you could not do on your own

mechanism the working parts of a machine

relax become looser

shock absorber mechanism in a vehicle that cushions the passengers from bumps and jolts

spokes metal wires or wooden rods that join the edge of a wheel to the hub in the middle

telescopes becomes shorter because one or more tubes slide inside another

tense tight

tension when something has a force acting on it

Answers to questions

p4 The long tight springs can be stretched but not squashed.

p5 Photo: Its weight and forward motion makes the end of the Slinky jump onto the step below, just as, when your foot trips over something, the rest of your body keeps moving forward until you hit the ground.

p5 The steps have to be the right depth and width for a Slinky to go all the way downstairs (and the Slinky needs to be placed in the middle of the step). A Slinky will not go upstairs, because it is the force of its weight which pulls it downstairs.

p9 Spongy rubber balls bounce higher than balls filled with air because they squash more when they hit the ground and store more of the **energy**.

p10 When you jump on a mattress, only the springs below and near your feet **compress**, but when you jump on a trampoline, all the springs around the edge stretch a little and so give you back more energy.

p12 To keep a door open you would have to fix a spring on the side of the door that you need to pull to open it.

p15 All the objects listed use springs except for the bookcase and xylophone.

p18 The girl is wearing an elasticated band in her hair, trousers with an elasticated waist, and is using a rubber band to hold the cards together.

p19 The further back you pull the rubber band, the further the car should go.

Index

Titles in the *How it Works* series include:

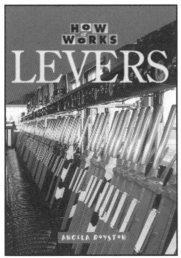

Hardback   0 431 01742 5

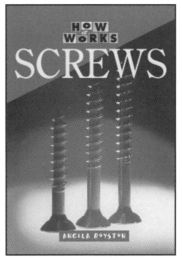

Hardback   0 431 01744 1

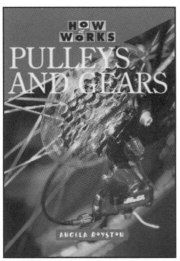

Hardback   0 431 01743 3

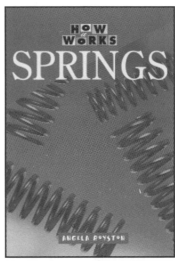

Hardback   0 431 01745 X

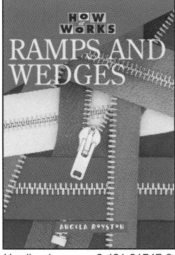

Hardback   0 431 01747 6

Hardback   0 431 01746 8

Find out about the other titles in this series on our website www.heinemann.co.uk/library